APPLES, APPLES EVERYWHERE!

Learning about Apple Harvests

by Robin Koontz

illustrated by Nadine Takvorian

PICTURE WINDOW BOOKS

a capstone imprint

Special thanks to our adviser for his expertise:

Terry Flaherty, Ph.D., Professor of English
Minnesota State University, Mankato

Shelly Lyons, editor; Lori Bye, designer
Nathan Gassman, art director; Jane Klenk, production specialist
The illustrations in this book were created digitally and with pencil.

Picture Window Books
1710 Roe Crest Drive
North Mankato, MN 56003
www.capstonepub.com

Library of Congress Cataloging-in-Publication Data
Koontz, Robin Michal.
Apples, apples everywhere! : learning about apple harvests / by Robin
Koontz ; illustrated by Nadine Takvorian.
p. cm. — (Autumn)
Includes index.
ISBN 978-1-4048-6012-4 (library binding)
ISBN 978-1-4048-6388-0 (paperback)
1. Apples—Harvesting—Juvenile literature. I. Takvorian, Nadine. II.
Title. III. Series: Autumn (Series) SB363.35.K66 2010
634'.11—dc22   2010000904

Plants are turning brown.

The air smells fresh.

It feels chilly.

It's not summer anymore.

Time to pick apples!

3

Wow! Look at all the apples!

At the apple orchard, trees sag with ripe fruit.

Welcome to our apple harvest.

Apples come in shades of red, yellow, or green.

Apples can be as small as a cherry.
They can be as big as a grapefruit.

Wow, that one's huge!

I got it!

In the orchard people are busy picking
and packing apples. Fruit ladders help
workers reach apples high in the tall trees.

9

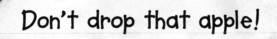

Workers put the apples in boxes. It's best to store apples in a cool place.

An apple rots quickly if it's bruised.

Apple worms live inside some apples. Apple worms are really moth caterpillars. The caterpillars eat the seeds and fruit.

Later they squirm their way out.

What's worse than finding a worm in your apple?
Finding half a worm.
Yuk!

Some apples taste tart. People like to use them for baking pies.

Sweet, crunchy apples are best for munching. Apples can be used for games too!

Let's bob for apples!

We can bob for apples because they float.

Cider is made from apples. First the fruit is crushed. Then the apple juice pours into a bucket.

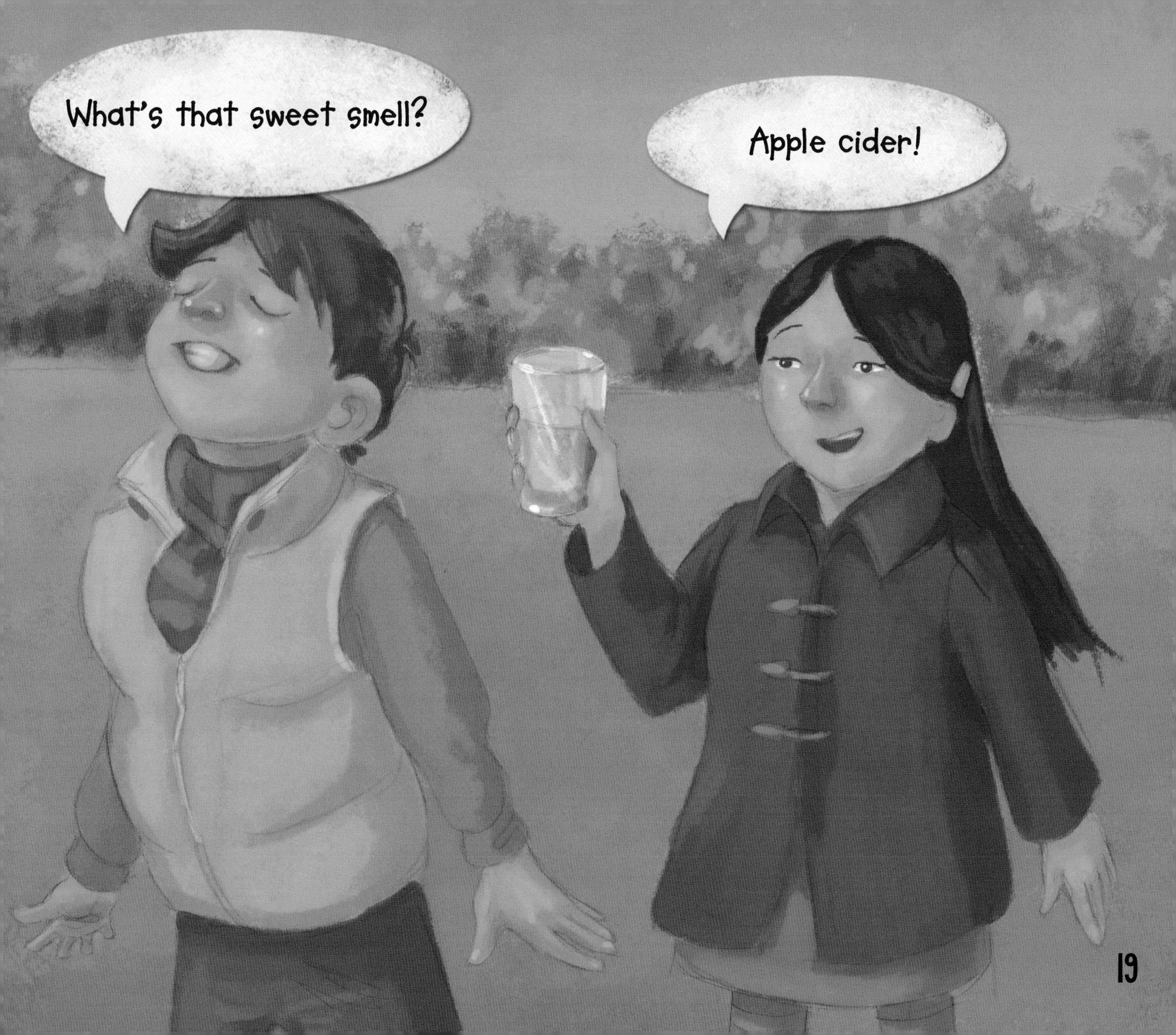
What's that sweet smell?
Apple cider!

People have harvested apples for thousands of years. It's fun to celebrate the apple harvest with others.

Dried Apple Wreath

What you need:

- Scissors
- Heavy-duty paper plate
- Crayons or markers
- Piece of heavy string or twine about 6 inches (15 centimeters) long
- Small branches of evergreen trees or shrubs
- Other dried materials such as seedpods, grasses, leaves, and cones
- White glue
- Dried apple rings from a store or homemade

What you do:

1. Cut a circle from the center of the paper plate to make a ring shape.
2. Color the paper ring as a background for your wreath.
3. Using the scissors, poke a small hole in the paper ring.
4. Put the string through the hole, and tie it in a loop. This is your wreath hanger.
5. Arrange small branches and dried materials around the ring shape.
6. When you like your design, glue the materials into place.
7. Let the glue dry.
8. Arrange the apple rings on top or in the spaces between the other materials.
9. Glue the apple rings into place and let them dry.
10. Hang up your wreath!

Glossary

autumn—the season of the year between summer and winter; autumn is also called fall

caterpillar—a wormlike animal that changes into a butterfly or moth; caterpillars hatch from eggs

cider—a drink made by pressing apples

harvest—the time or season when fruits and vegetables are ready for picking

orchard—a field of fruit or nut trees

ripe—ready to pick and eat

tart—tasting sour, not sweet

More Books to Read

Esbaum, Jill. *Apples for Everyone*. Picture the Seasons. Washington, D.C.: National Geographic, 2009.

McNamara, Margaret. *Picking Apples*. Ready to Read: Robin Hill School. New York: Aladdin Paperbacks, 2009.

Nelson, Robin. *Apple Trees*. First Step Nonfiction: Plant Life Cycles. Minneapolis: Lerner Publications, 2008.

Slade, Suzanne. *From Seed to Apple Tree: Following the Life Cycle*. Amazing Science: Life Cycles. Minneapolis: Picture Window Books, 2009.

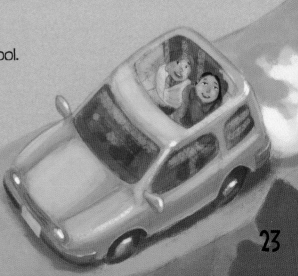

Internet Sites

FactHound offers a safe, fun way to find Internet sites related to this book. All of the sites on FactHound have been researched by our staff.

Here's all you do:
Visit www.facthound.com
FactHound will fetch the best sites for you!

Index

Check out all the books in the Autumn series:

Apples, Apples Everywhere!: Learning about Apple Harvests
Busy Animals: Learning about Animals in Autumn
Leaves Fall Down: Learning about Autumn Leaves
Pick a Perfect Pumpkin: Learning about Pumpkin Harvests